The Wardrobe Mistress

The Wardrobe Mistress

Beatriz Hausner

Ekstasis Editions

National Library of Canada Cataloguing in Publication Data

Hausner, Beatriz,
    The Wardrobe Mistress

    Poems.
    ISBN 1-894800-24-9

    I. Title.
    PS8577.E4T43 2002   C811'.54   C2002-910335-5
    PR9199.3.N37T43 2002

© Beatriz Hausner 2003
Cover Art: Susana Wald

Published in 2003 by:
Ekstasis Editions Canada Ltd.   Ekstasis Editions
Box 8474, Main Postal Outlet   Box 571
Victoria, B.C. V8W 3S1   Banff, Alberta T0L 0C0

The Wardrobe Mistress has been published with the assistance of grants from the Canada Council and the Cultural Services Branch of British Columbia.

For Arni Brownstone

Contents

THE WARDROBE MISTRESS

The Wardrobe Mistress	11
Byzantine Date	13
Down	15
This Side of the Styx	16
Emigrant	17
Ars Poetica	19
My Man Loss	20

DOMESTIC TREATISES

Domestic Treatises	23
Rubens' Cat	24
My New Bag	26
Coppelius and His Doll	27

THE ARCHIVAL EDUCATION

Enter the Librarians	33
The Query	36
Man, Woman, Machine	37
Je ne mange pas de ce pain là	38
The Archival Education	39
The Double Life	41
Telephone Duty	43
The Interviews	45
Curl Up and Dye	47

ETHNOLOGY OF THE BEDROOM

Time for Cats	51
Streetcar Madness	53
Northern Plains	56
The Empty Bed	58
Rhythm and Blues Method	59
The Wild Life	60
Ethnology of the Bedroom	61
There Is a Great Bubble	62
Rabbit Passion	63
Magritte's Lovers in Toronto	64
Dancer	65

I

The Wardrobe Mistress

The Wardrobe Mistress

The mistress enters
the wardrobe finds her garments
are ripe fruits neatly stacked
seasonal limbs plucked

handed down from the grand
mothers who stitched the heart.
Lady of fittings she stumbles on hooks
and eyes keepers of the herring

bone collar of inverted pleats falling
down the neckline of last year's
required dress hollowed-out
tree recumbent the beloved

smiles from his bed of stone.
Breathless the mistress opens
the chest of drawers silk kimonos
beckon from a field of red

shoes that thirst for feet
attacked by mobs on horseback
galloping counterclockwise
to the river that crosses the man

from sleeve to sleeve.
His cats dismount.
Emblematic buttons precede
the temperamental fingers

of his hands guests of the cross-
stitch: longing at the seams
she overcomes her timeless corsets
and shoots contour darts.

The mistress stands by
her wardrobe determines
the position of pant legs
centered zippers on velvet

jackets that weigh down
the reality of her skirts.
She conjures buttonholes
for her lover: may his tongue

weave its coral into her.
Razor-sharp his voice rises
up the pastoral expanses of her
legs released the tucks of his ancestors

smile from bygone bell-bottoms.
Weft and warp the eyelets
join at the root where first
man and woman are sewn

to each other by love's elastic
needles. Bound once released
the mistress reaches deep within
the wardrobe weeping then

locks it throws away the key.

Byzantine Date

He invited her for coffee
in Constantinople. He claimed
he could not drink through
his mouth that cups were meant
for wearing on one's feet.

She swooned at his imaginative
designs pictured him covered
in petals shaped like hearts.
He maintained that coffee
was better in an oriental setting
witness to past civilizations.

In her confusion she mistook her soul
for that of the goddess of love a new
Aphrodite whose modern breasts belied
the tingling ghost of Theodora.

She floated in at the agreed time
her heart ticking with
the insufferable hands of clocks
echoing the howls of men
who shout prayers through megaphones.

Inverted Rapunzel she counted
the bricks on the towering minarets
casting the shadows of past centuries
on the cooling coffee.
"Late as usual," she thought.

The years turned her golden
dress to rust her hair to ash.
Tired of waiting she slowly raised
her gaze and saw her shadows moving away.

As she rose to go she felt her skin
sagging and foreign and resigned
to the inevitable denouement she accepted
that he had, in fact, stood her up.

Down

Gather your parts in the morning:
they have been served and lie at your feet
as you get off the bed and realize
that the room is full of claws and shadows
growing gray under your feet: above
the sky is slate and cold air. Inside outside
the furniture moves with the wind howling
in the corners of winter which grows roots
in the foundations of the only house.

No one is behind you yet someone follows
his shadow prolonging your darkness
as you enter the rigidity of the clock
where the lines are straight driving
the fury which fills the ancestral bundles.

Somewhere deep inside the shards of laughter
pierce the darkness. Your ghosts clamor to get out
leave the sealed boxes invent a new phoenix of flesh
and blood enter the sun.

This Side of the Styx

I will build a boat from your bones
push against the bottom with a long pole
made of a tree felled by ghosts
ferry myself to the middle of the pond
liquid body made from your eyes.

A suffused green light polishes
the darkness of this landscape where your
image suddenly beckons from the far shore.
You are iridescent in death you play
among dry grasses disappear into the rolling hills.

On the other bank some would call the shore of the living
where the stone feels cold and humidity grows
ice roots, I draw the Styx out of my sex
and pull the boat of death and life to this side of the pond.

Emigrant
for Joseph Hausner

Love with the skin without it.
Inside the heart is a burrow
where the ancestors visit
their animals knotted body and soul.

In the new country
seek the original fruit.
It is found
        nestled among sounds.
Found
        like a seed
        strumming the edges of being.
Found where
        the word lies ready
        orchestral families rising from
        the ink
        distilled
        moon
        clock
        secret
        numbers and codes.

We were overcome by various
selves living in the guitar
electric liquid on the tongue as
I leaped into the honey jars and tasted
the walls of the kingdom of bees.

Imagined and real new lands
reverberated on my pillows:

        silent steps of the doe caught
        by trees black against snow—

    a gloved hand running
    up my newcomer's back—

    the host spider drawing its web from
    tears crossed by black crows.

Pain of remembering the mountains.
An invisible hand working
the brain where the eternal
house slowly ceases before ancestral
ash of wandering flame alive
under changing skies:
strangeness renews its gritty touch.

Ars Poetica

> *Qué bonita es la música.*
> —Elíades Ochoa

The word is in the mouth
acquainted with keys in the
closed hand the letters float
A and C and B driving
the punctuation meltdown.
The eyes gaze from the screen.
They observe the motion of words
with shoes walking the country

of music furnished souls that
grow fruits without ending that fall
from windows waterfalls
of utterances softening the edges
your landscapes breathe.

The song of warm ice echoes the
proverbial surface where the sun
rises and sets its animals running
wild when I lie down and wrap
myself in woolen flowers.
The Orient screams out the penultimate
rhyme absolute dominion of old moss
growing between your legs source
of all sounds this heart. Your armies
their terrible workers release the voice.

Without nails to claw out its demotic
patterns the voice draws lines on the
snow where my ghosts stitch the trail
for the trees to grow roots of song.

My Man Loss

One day loss moved into my body
grew limbs hands with fingers to press
at my heart metal fingernails to poke
at my insides. Long rattling sounds
rose with the snake at the core my veins
growing heavy with all those dead.

Burdened by itself loss moved
into the house of dream. Once there
he began to appear to me nightly
attired in dark suits, assuming other
personalities for my crumbling occasions.

One dark night loss sat at my desk
began to write about a long corridor
beneath the foundations of my house
there where gauze covered the skeletons.

I sat on the knees of loss pointed
to silence, spoke to him about my country
its rivers its dependencies its amphibious
tongues that enter leave the drawers
of these dark furnishings.

Time has passed. Sorrow now
has me bound to the tree of
childhood whose limbs grow inward.

Etched on bark, loss's face appears,
his eyes return to their sockets his mouth
still detached speaks to me of days
spent frightening the predators in
the woods where we finally are, I his
Rapunzel, he my Knight, insomniac
and alone with his detached body parts.

II

Domestic Treatises

Domestic Treatises

The lady of the house is
an immense love sectioned into
rooms that turn into themselves.

She cleans utterly becomes one
with the dust entering the collective
mind she vacuums corners lets in the air
through windows languid with neglect.

Several eternities of interlocking
hinges tear at her soul. Poor
lady of the bath servant of tyrannical
faucets and tiles she readies herself
for the onslaught of her critical guests.

The perfect wife seeks and finds a couch
with legs that wane and wax rooms of
flexible chintzes self-cleaning knick
knacks loving offspring no mess.

She unlocks her cleaners polishes
sideboards while her nails grow.
Symphonic brushes sweep her wireless
brain: she envisions a country with
mirrors for her unfurnished sorrow.

The housewife pulls the strings of her
fortified fingers draws out her heart spreads
it over the matrimonial bed now covered
with swallows maybe hens reminders
of summer's distant cackle when
she sang her angles into neat curves.

Rubens' Cat
for Ludwig Zeller

Rubens' cat is tired
exhausted from entering
and leaving the alphabet
soup. Fed up and sleepy
she grows a mechanical
arm from her ribs.

The cat is sad. Soft glass
spilled over the eye
her boxes began to speak.
The ideal daughter is hot:
a fishhook trains her ear
her head wears shoes.

The painter appears.
His ladies wave gestures
and reveal their magic powders
to the minute-counting cat
who lives inside the couch.
She travels the floor on her finger
nails hangs from the lamps.

The cat is a housewife who
believes in the ritual organization
of jars which feed her
necklaces. She's arranged
her soul in concentric circles
with their center where
the master lives with the night.
A rough darkness sets in.
Her feline soul grows more exacting.

She is learning the preparation
of medium-sized prey for her
young who creep up the trees
where her phosphorescent
fathers once lived. The cat
exists on an elastic screen
clings to the exclusive
territory of current events
served proudly on a dish by
Rubens who works the pulleys
of her chairs and licks her
geometric feet.

Furious the cat searches out
her elders who get lost
in the endless typographic
forest where her toys lie abandoned
relics of that domestic beyond
where her kittens meow.

My New Bag

Brown outside silky
brown inside the new
bag came in the mail
neatly folded I opened its
edges and discovered my
dependents had installed
their landscapes of water
and earthen surfaces gifts
for this heart fed by arctic rivers.

Now that it's spring swallows
fly in and out of the bag of
forest leaves. I enter and begin
my daily walk down its zippers
into a pocket which opens into
prairies where chiefs
who threaten to poison
the contents of my bag
live in chains.

Many legs burst out of my bag
as we rush down the street
emptying our fires our pleasure.
Formerly stored in its corners my
selves delve deeper into the bag
where the little people are delicate
despite their habit-acquired love
of living with big cats inside
my brand new bag.

Coppelius and His Doll

> *There was something measured and stiff about her gait and posture that struck many people as unpleasant, but was attributed to a feeling of constraint due to the social occasion.*
> —E.T.A. Hoffmann

Coppelius went looking for the great eye
but found the doll Olympia her limbs
scattered at the dream fair. He shed layers
of skin uncovered his scientific bones
took her various parts home in a car
pulled by the hungry dogs
of loneliness and rain pelting his insides.

Coppelius spent his days
blowing into the mouth
piecing together the disparate parts of
the new wife. Watched over by beavers
he bolted in limbs attached eyes
mobile lids painted her remaining
features with his blood.

I return you to your musical instruments
burrow deep within pianos touch the keys
glimpse your secrets hidden with your garments
in the wardrobe made of skin. Author of your days
I will use desire's alphabet to define the syntax
of your tongue will hover above you
watch surfaces sweeten your sex.

The doll stood up conjured her ghostly
extremities the joints fell into sync.
Alive at last Olympia felt the cats
stir in her country of dew and dark humus.
Lit from inside her eyes now filled the
sockets moist finally with unspoken vision
latent in her mouth. Her tongue grew hard
her palate awakened to the taste
of the immemorial tea of childhood fevers.
Her nails turned solid fingertips
opened to touch inertia gave way as she
reached out to her creator: daughter of Coppelius
conjuring the tingling stairs of her new house
furnished with abounding white linens.

I come alive on your mirrored brow
new circuitry drives my pleasure
from edge to edge as you place your hand
on my back winding up the key so this metal
heart may beat rhythmically systole-diastole
love pushes movement into toes into feet
alive to the wiring of your electric
tongue while the clocks shift inside
their shrunken casements I who am invented
by you finally arrive to our symphony of
mad cuckoos screaming their song tingling
these legs swivel in their sockets
as I ride you piercing me enormously
to the heart shaking and with my knees rooted
to the bed you pushing my back further
into my spine my neck folding into digits
incoherence of the mechanical spasms.

Coppelius and his doll surrendered
their sections moved to and fro with their limbs.
Reborn always spinning threads they wove
themselves into the crackling starches of the bed
their shared screams filling empty shoes of past
lives: the lamps trembled. Exhausted Coppelius
and his doll dismissed their ghosts to live out
the eternal dream of their nuptials.

III

The Archival Education

Enter the Librarians

The streets of Alexandria are full
of claws. The library beckons
its suns and moons break
with insects in the heat
seeping from languid scrolls.

The daughters of Ptolemy wear
down their nails. They are a
sisterhood obedient pilgrims
condemned to endless elastic
marble which rises vertically
like skin inscribed with hieroglyphs
never deciphered poor
obsessed classifiers.

Besieged the great library
opens its doors to knotted sleep
while its columns crumble
and the earth unlocks its vaults to
millions of tomes restrained by
mobs of slow moving words.

                        The library
seeks its meanings within.
The professionals recite
the scriptures in reverse order
old initiates of nonsense they
feel their way through the
dust which thickens
into ready-made boxes.

Indexers of the labyrinth they
live for a taxonomy of moans
praying for the beyond while
their souls settle down to wait
for a country of windows and doors.

The librarians dissolve
into complicated robes they
cry ink tears they scratch at
the edges of knowledge dig
with tongues into the mire
and pull out their scalded
shrieks from the Egyptian sea
where scribes once planted
verbal flowers in their ears.

Rendered blind by centuries
of lists the specialists gather
they discuss the viability of teeth
an instant numerology for the countries
their spiritual grandmothers once roamed.

The sisters are plodding but timely
followers of the discipline of shelves
they qualify their suitors to death
bemoan the solitude of old
daguerreotypes the seed
of love classed under the same
helpless number which never cools.
In their hands meaning dies.

Bearing gifts the women approach
the clients in the eight hundreds
rising from turning chairs
their toneless mantra greets
Melvil Dewey's decapitated
self cast in plaster
his Nineteenth Century
soul redolent of dogs.

"Oh great one of the duodecimal
reveal your points" they implore
but the waterfall of numbers
suddenly buries hope and
though they struggle to preserve
the image of His Face the great
library disappears in the dusty
stones of the streets of Alexandria.

The Query

There are no real questions
to these answers like coils
smiling their mellifluous
echoes shaping the eternal
question whispered in song.

The exhausted scribe twists.

"Repeat your question," she
asks, but the ungiving
apparatus between her and her
inquisitor becomes a tree
whose invisible roots move
her arms and legs, branches
which end in hooks that seek
a response from clocks
forever stuck on the hour.

The questioner returns,
demands to know the exact
volume of wonder in
the waters that line his nation.
"This is your answer," she offers,
glowing, daily rising from ash
expanding with her silent ancestors

gasping. Her generational
despair is sacred and subsists
with unspoken memories which
rush down lengthening her capillaries
humming and slowing the grind
as they etch the letters on stone
and announce a new world
of pictures uttered through lips
tightened skin forcing the song.

Man, Woman, Machine

When man approaches the machine
he imagines woman made of squares
and digits, her mouth soundless and moist.

Stars appear. The keys multiply, curve
into a soundless universe where man
hums the tune of desire sudden and restless.

Speaking in foreign tongues he digs
a new foundation for the tower of Babel
while his armies leave the motherland behind.

When woman approaches the machine her love
recoils into outlets where it lives on the edge with noise.
Mad queen bee she employs machine and imagines

her fruit slowly transformed into finished delicacies
which she quarters like an interminable body of
uncooked flesh. Prisoner of its functions woman

delights at the efficiency of machine, celebrates
sucking noises of her mechanical companion
as they travel the expanding universe of her home.

When machine approaches man and woman,
subjects of disunity, it wanders lost pounding
its anger at plastic surfaces, screaming out complaints

at its wireless instruments that replace childhood
with the melancholy of dark omens perpetual
metals that explode in the night. It cries

longing for that first happiness, the spectacular
moment contained in the peals of laughter of mothers
and fathers at play in the first country of happiness.

Je ne mange pas de ce pain là

I once worked for a cruel woman.
Angry and tired she grew hoarse
in her silence while we shouted
our complaint to the tutelary
gods of the workplace weaving
our tears into elaborate garments.

New demonic Alice, her elastic neck
hung over us as she served the bitter
meal of twisted shrunken limbs. She
excelled at preparing elaborate dishes
whose assembly she followed obediently
from a book of rules inscribed
by invisible fat superiors whose metal claws
she dutifully polished until they glowed.

Time has passed. Today, I sometimes see
her eyes gazing at me from the soup
I carefully stir in my worst nightmares.

The Archival Education

Poised for a periodic division of the world
the archivist measures her fingernails
classifies her place treading backward

the waters push her to the edge.
She pretends that the one who governs
does not place her parts inside boxes

with casters that her bleating animals
still roam the galleries of her museum where the chief
from hell shouts his commands

while filing down his metal claws.
The archivist dreams. She grades the
beloved's sudden eyes labels his tongue

follows the ancient grid where they once
set their clocks merged their records
combined breaths insufflated life into

documents long ago drafted in secret.
She understands his alphabetic
armies supports them as they take the high

ground beyond beloved limits
where the senses intervene repeatedly playing
tauromachy with classification numbers.

She is not alone in Kafka's castle
the hallways succumb to flocks of birds
flying in and out of mouths

the shelves open close mechanical
furniture expanding the rubber walls
to fit the bloating selves of directors

dancing up and down the hierarchy.
Cautiously the archivist crawls out
to her sphere shouts and grows hoarse

as invisible levers speed up the heavy grind.
Ranting against her tools she splits
herself in two seals the boxes

begins to live the hermetic life.

The Double Life

> *They say, sing while you save, but I just get bored.*
> —Bob Dylan

The office worker stands
upside down, her hair a mop
for cleaning words forsaken
of filing cabinets. She speaks
of doing it on an imaginary
rug but the eternal supervisor
is tone deaf and yawns.

Secretary of tutelary gods
she places her eyes on the desk
feels the cool air entering her
darkness, speedily finding
the edges of her losses.
Her brain growing
purple petals close
to the nerve computes the
glimmers of iridescences.

The nightmare ebbs
and flows depending on
the punctuality of the engine
that drives her fingers over keys.
She imagines a sudden country
of flowers that are bells suspended
midair calling her to her true
home of moist prairies
and open skies.

The outside is not
the inside: her desk
assaults the office worker once again
as she sinks back into a chair
that swivels and spins out
of control. Windows
that do not open, inaudible voices
and dead fish are set before her
so she may turn them into paper
for building the walls that isolate
her from her love.

A sudden phone crowds
her senses, intermittent
acoustics pull the strings
inside the ears calling the eyes
back to their sockets so the
dormant terrible worker
can return to working
the miracle of the double life.

Telephone Duty

The woman is connected at
the ears. Memories enter her phonic
universe pushing at the pendulum
of moods in full regalia her suitors
dance through the headset
mechanical ambassadors of deceit

Receptionist of quotidian gods
she greets her oral guests
with careful enunciation steals
their thoughts with her tongue
while a third hand waters
the garden blooming there
where her legs meet the chair.

She adjusts the volume between
calls her soul expectant
of the beloved's approach
retreats. Ever-present he walks
over the cordless Styx. Enticing
his gifts are majestic
and made of stillness.

On the screen his image suddenly
reminds her of nether-eyes
touching speaking in tongues
phosphorescent cats spring
to life in the black mouth
where the digits beckon.

No longer on hold despicable
managers weed all pleasure from the line
while inside her ear the spider weaves
corners etched long ago by love.

They buried the receiver in her
brain and now work the erasure
so the tribe of cannibal fish may enter:
they alone understand the extension
of the tiger's stripes from their
ideal location at the other end.

Ecstatic the phone hostess
presses keys tunes her ear to those
meteors shifting in their orbits as they
crash into the glowing heart choking
the line that connects her to
ghostly lovers in the beyond.

The Interviews

Working girl
pumps up the leopard
skin hat readies
her fingernails
to go meet
the relentless interviewer.

Momentarily
she forgets that
she's walking
neurotic dogs
that wear high
heels and corsets
of self-pity.

Her fear is timely.
The room is dead.
She's poised.

The questions
come down sewn
in velvet but she can't
hear them. Her brain
is constructed
backwards.

Luck enters.
Her inner keyboard
begins to work.
Black letters
pour out
of her mouth
dissolve as they touch
the gulf between
her and the inquisitor
who remains
invisible to the
working girl's eyes:
her gaze faces
inward where
her interviewer
is holding firmly
to his pen writing
out her sentence
in blood.

Curl Up and Dye

"Your hair curls sideways," she said.
The mirror cracked vertically
a paw waved through the fissure
flags announced your arrival
years of absence and dew
covered your fur sweet cat
my cat: you are here.

You wrap me in silks
the hairdresser shrieks
chairs swivel out of control you
are fire in the coldest day kindling
the wound you run sharp nails down
my back blood rises and I feel
the night swallowing us while
the professionals form a circle.

Ours is this carnival the spectators
hold their combs the moon turns
the sun shows its teeth. Let us
continue the party has just begun
skilled hands shake the floor
the lamps in the mirror spin
your stripes envelop me: I am made
invisible while the others forget
we are alone on grass that is cool
that is fresh your weight
solace of warm stars inside these
walls you gather your vertebrates.

My cat, purr, speak to me:
The curling iron is growing restless.

IV

Ethnology of the Bedroom

Time for Cats

I feel your steps: clickity clack
on the floor the electric touch
of whiskers on lips eminence
of your designs: here are my feet.

Let's meet on treetops grow
used to unfamiliar grounds
summon our warm-blooded
selves hang from the lamps
untangle the wires stuck between
our teeth so the heart can grow warm.

Our limbs quicken the pace
I glimpse fast scissors
in your eyes cut-out landscapes
doors of disbelief frame us
while search parties seek you out
in jungles of furniture your feline
ancestors drop their spots into a cup.

The curtains breathe
in out
and threaten to eat us alive.
I put my ear on your chest
an echoing room reverberates.
The birds are perched
on your arms morning light
and dew gather on your eyelids.

Tiger your fur lines
these walls pleasure sharpens
these fingernails it plucks at your stripes
I am your servant. Tirelessly I go
to the well and draw the living heart
beat that marks the hour so
fragments of anxiety may grow
in the throat and the tongue
swallow itself with your image.

Let's be to the power of nine
our lives will purr to the harmony
of two bodies. We'll burrow together
until you waken my interiors until
our bones glow under bed sheets.
We'll leave my tongue in the wardrobe
whose key is lost.

Streetcar Madness
for Susana Wald

I ate my kitty's paws. The tail too.
On a streetcar I devoured him
bite by bite front to back stalled
traffic whizzing by we sat

beating our hearts into
edible heat. At the lights
we reclined the seats sighed
rolled towards a humid

station climbed the backbone
of madness spied an enormous eye
grew elegant lips. Our knees met
at the top of the escalator.

The merry citizens lived out
their secrets inside the briefcase fruit
moaned fish longed for the ocean
cool pleasure water filled

the change box. My kitty licked
his whiskers and settled on the armrest.
Instantly the driver's raw voice
turned on my windows jealousy

filled the air teeth rattled
softly sinking into vinyl
seats your carnivores made
the lady passenger in me

blush. Words expired
caught in the jaws.
At the next stop we switched
to the express lanes raced

toward the authority of the clock
which died when we rang the bell
our baggage began to bloom.
Hide, cat. When your goodness

exits strange eyes will fill
the distance between your fingertips
and my tongue. Other ghosts will sit
next to me wearing

sunflower masks one thousand
eyes will search out the closed landscape.
Invisible inside your briefcase
I eat the libidinous apple.

My unessential pasts are put
to rest and soon the streetcar comes to
a halt. Inflections pronounce your stripes.
Let's play hide and seek I will find

you upside down in the corner
and with my nails wear down your
linings. Locomotion is maddening.
Artificial jungles grow inside

the rearview mirror. Seated standing
the travelers sweat ink.
Where is the true cat? I sense your
breathing approaching bearing

gifts the wireless letter grows
roots back in my garden.
Let's climb on the roof.
Once the others wilt we'll hang

from a glance and watch your skylights
while the woman inside
uncovers a basket overflowing
with eyes for you for me.

Northern Plains

I lie surrounded by inverted
landscapes where the sun is the heart
setting inside the mouth. Night falls.
I dream of your head radiant
stillness between my hands.

Drawing sound out of you I place
my landscapes next to your ear
so you may listen to the slow waters
flowing at the center of our house
where echoes of my childhood
surrender to the imperial mountains.

The room is cold the walls watch
anxiety and its shadows fall
on pillows I dig with my teeth
conjure your chest and listen
to the distant breathing of the ancestors
their bones crackling under ash and snow.

Tired servant of wakefulness I brush
dew off our eyes go to the well
draw up the waters of sleep.
They will cover the cold stones
the edges of longing. Listen now:
their nuptial sounds announce
a new country of windows and doors.

My skin bristles from waiting.
I sleep in the chamber of melancholy here
where invisible hands collect fragments of images
of you and your tongue swallowing
itself plucked from the tree of pleasure.

Let's dissolve into darkness follow
the trail of stars through fingertips
rebuild the world. Its disjointed
parts grate against the night
which expands ceaselessly filling
our bed with iridescent animals.

I open my eyes: dark branches fill
the room the tiger made of mirrors
rises before me its deceitful likeness
indisputable and alive on your brow.

The Empty Bed

Awake the eyes open
touch the salty linens beating
against my sides bringing me
your surfaces renewed like blood
etching a beginning for each letter
of your name in my mouth
imperfect to describe you without
your limbs in full attendance.

Motionless landscape white
on white lodged in your tongue
I find a stone pleasure your face
shifting semblance of the mirror
breaking above us as we
appropriate the night.

I surrender my country
all its dependencies and my
veins lay tribute at your feet so
my heart may outgrow this body.

My prince of utterances you
whose roots lie upended and undeniable.

Impatience sets in. Shadows
in conversation with smaller
beasts whose hides cannot compete
with those of your herds. Dry rustling
of leaves on the beach of this ocean
where the eminent sounds
of our music die surrounded by
translucent ermines returning me
to this walled fortress without sleep.

Rhythm and Blues Method

Negotiations are ongoing.
The fallopian cadre answers
signals requests breaks longer
than the minute-counting managers
will allow. The interpretation
of contractual language belies a new
syntax for the heart beating in the
belly where the nerves find their center.

Wait, wait—they say. A pause
is in order. The workers are good
they keep perfect attendance they
are timely. At body central
the floors tremble on the tenth
day contracting out woman's
essence to pleasure. An onslaught
of emotion and tears of joy override
all existing agreements. The great
arbitrator always speaks through the flesh.

The Wild Life

Let us count backward
forward test the nerves
for you to feel the hot flame
inside our box of secrets.

Red-winged blackbirds
nest on your tongue
between teeth
my sweet I cling to
your cruel stripes
a fluttering of wings
up and down my spine.

I am growing roots
the miserly trees that crowd
my nights grow wild inside
your armpits I will bury
my breath and the warm earth
will speak to me of you
while I weave with your heart
strings a tight noose
around my throat.

Ethnology of the Bedroom

Between you and me there is the night
swallowing the bed without stopping
we leave your shadows at the door and
enter the trail of stars that grows from your fingers.

Let's become equal to the sounds
rising from the place where
your tongue touches the pillow
follows the silk of the panther

between us. Its soft fur swells
I hear its breathing I retreat
terrified of enemy voices while
you shout your song electric

dissonance makes the birds in the
drawers sing the dying light on
prairie linens extends our love
into horse country a new Montana

in conversation with our bed.
We gallop along the edges of
the Appaloosa's spots our own
and secret constellation.

There Is a Great Bubble

There is a great bubble
in my heart a primitive
emptiness lodged between stocking
and leg calling my extremities
to play at being and non-being.

The current impasse of man
woman and bed are an open
sea for paper-pressed
kisses and aardvarks.
My dearest is fast approaching
the edge of the plank.

The bubble is the
beginning and the end
eternal surrogate of a
northern plain where my
horsemen roam free: to the heart
to the heart—they shout.
The enemy stops

places his ear close and
listens to the waves breaking
inside and the secret is revealed:
there is an ocean inside the bubble
where fish swim with your eyes.

Rabbit Passion
for Veronica Brownstone

Walking up the stairs I meet a large
rabbit lavender pelt and lavender teeth
seduce like purple fiction pouring
from the mouth which spells "R" first letter
of an alphabet for rabbits. He inquires

about my latest search for a ghost
with fur whose main occupation
is the care of other rabbits traveling
daily to jobs in offices for invisible
lavender-colored rabbits. They break
at noon and visit a great number

of cousins of the lavender rabbit
lurching in the background where
the rodent grandmothers purvey
roots and cabbage leaves concurrent
with the diet for lovers of furry animals
whose bones glow under manic cotton tails

earlier versions of the lavender
rabbit descending the staircase.

Magritte's Lovers in Toronto

The lovers exchanged mouths
through the rough weave of
their shrouds. The music

poured out of a suitcase: fire
and water, a universe inside
a square box with latches. They

stood, their feelings behind them
Magritte's own anniversary
a rock of pigment on canvas

beyond their immediate
location. Magritte's lovers
leaned on folded umbrellas

ready for rain in a sunny day
waterfall of crystal as backdrop.
They moved in Toronto every

fifteen minutes breathed deeply
into one another vowing to change
the world in that one kiss

communicating vessels their
bodies standing firm on the seed

Dancer

Red yellow feathers paradise
of doors fingernails cleaving
the Plains. The rider lives
inside the drum his horse cuts
the landscape cathedral of speed
fast approaching echo
plucking at my metals, vibrations
in the closed mouth.

We walk the rope, dancer,
my edges gasp they drown in sweetgrass
hot ribbon placed over obstacles:
our armies leap to the dance.
A guttural voice calls in the wind
polishes the black surface of the Face.

They have bolted the mirrors.
Dust follows the beauty of those purple furs
ripe thistles separate your hemispheres
when you dismount the ground gives way
to your feet lined with beaded landscapes.

Thunder breaks the bones
on the tensed skin the body works
its wheels, it proclaims
the descent of your bundles
hurting seed that splinters the soil
deep down where we lie silent and wait
for the swan to sail across the brow.

The ancestors arrive
your headdress comes undone
the feathers grow they enter
the sinews and reach beyond

limbs that crowd your steps.
Blood rises, you become
a plumed dream of flames
when you jump from the horse.

More wondrous than Elias in his car
you drive the whirlwind of colored
grasses which nurture my ghosts.
Pleasure and pain, vivid plumes curve
your back. Elastic and tense
                                        we dance
oblivious to the thunder of mechanical
hooves that tear apart the prairie mantle.

In your hand the beating heart beckons:
open your wings to a reddened sky of suns.